The Maine Coon's Haiku

The Maine Coon's Haiku

and Other Poems for Cat Lovers

Michael J. Rosen

illustrated by
Lee White

CANDLEWICK PRESS

Inside

Maine Coon

Ragdoll

Turkish Angora

Siamese

Russian Blue

Maine Coon

crouched before the couch,
suddenly, cat has all night
for just one sound: mouse

Ragdoll

why today the cat
who sleeps beneath the ivy
halved the blameless hearts

Turkish Angora

whooshing down the hall:
Angora, then her all-white
dust devil of hair

Siamese

a toppled lamp shade

moon moth must be here somewhere

batted from the dark

Russian Blue

blue-gray window frost

blue-gray shadowed room—lone square

of sun: blue-gray cat

Outside

Bombay

Norwegian Forest Cat

British Shorthair

American Shorthair

Burmese

Bombay

paired shadows prowling
in nightfall, but just two lights
pierce that darkness

Norwegian Forest Cat

caught among branches

fog descends the trunk headfirst

one foot at a time

British Shorthair

paws plant mud-daisies
along the polished hillside
parked on the cat's street

Store

American Shorthair

outside the old store
more strays sun as the screen door
bangs—bangs shut, again

Burmese

only the blazing
forsythia blooms rival
the Burmese cat's gaze

Inside

Birman

Balinese

Himalayan

Japanese Bobtail

Abyssinian

Birman

up to bat again
white-mitted kitten *hits! runs!*
fields! slides into home!

Balinese

on the windowsill's
balance beam, the cat pirouettes
as the kibble pings

Himalayan

spring's dew-heavy grass
prints climb the stairs, each fainter—
ghost cats haunt the house

Japanese Bobtail

captured behind glass,
one half asleep, one half price,
antique-store bobtails

WELCOME

Abyssinian

curled up on your book
cat won't care what happens next
now's the only page

Outside

Persian

Havana Brown

Scottish Fold

Bengal

Manx

Persian

stiff, winter-white cat
still pads the snow-hidden path
all is mute as flakes

Havana Brown

sun-baked umbrella
iced-tea glass sweats, pools—first drip
wakes the sleeping cat

Scottish Fold

wind-whipped magnolia
cat's pink-petal toes—the last
to drop from its boughs

Bengal

Bengal paces yard . . .
neighbors' yards . . . block—nowhere near
wild, nowhere near tame

Manx

two stories higher
stretched flat along the porch rail:
manx, the setting sun

Maine Coon

It's not true that a raccoon mated with a Maine farm cat to create the Maine coon—even though the brown tabby of this breed *does* have the striped tail of a 'coon and even though these cats *do* have a broad-chested, thick-haired body and can weigh up to twenty pounds.

A gentle, bushy-tailed giant, the Maine coon is the first long-haired cat to arise naturally in the United States. (That means that the cats themselves, rather than humans, selected their mates.)

Not lap sitters, these cats "chirp" contentedly throughout the day, roaming a farm or even walking on leashes in the city. Maine coons once traveled as mousers aboard ships, which may explain why they like curling up in small spaces and frolicking in water.

Ragdoll

Bred in California about fifty years ago—from the mating of Birman and Persian parents—ragdolls are so easygoing and attached to their humans that they hardly mind being handled, carried, or fussed over. Substantial cats with silky, medium-length fur and a large, long, muscular body, they are born white and develop color and pattern over their first few years.

Intelligent and easy to train, ragdolls will fetch, come, and sit. They're "people cats," perfect for cat people.

The haiku was inspired by my cat Slinky, who enjoyed snoozes beneath a particular begonia for years until, one day, for no reason I could discern, she shredded the plant's pendulous leaves. *Did they suddenly inch too close, Slinky?*

Turkish Angora

Five hundred years ago, there were no long-haired cats in Europe. The first to arrive hailed from Turkey. When these Angora cats began to be bred with other cats, that Angora look persisted: slender face, brilliant eyes, and a gorgeous, long, solid-color coat.

With britches (a feathering of longer hairs) on the rear legs and a well-plumed tail, the white Angora—the classic look—often has eyes of different colors.

Especially in warm parts of the world, the long-haired Turkish Angora sheds so much of its coat in summer that it actually resembles a short-haired cat.

Siamese

The Siamese may be the most recognizable cat breed, with its sapphire-blue, almond-shaped eyes; sleek build; mewling or yowling voice; and pale, solid coat with darker tail, ears, feet, and lower face—a look known as color-pointed.

Siamese princesses (*Siam* is a former name for Thailand) entrusted their many rings to their cats, sliding the bands onto their tails. Royal breeders worked to create cats with kinked or corkscrew tails just to keep the rings from sliding off. Likewise, it was thought that these cats carried the immortal souls of ancient royalty.

Siamese cats tend to be unpredictable, persistent, and meddlesome (prying open cabinets and demanding attention), but these traits seem only to endear them to their devoted following.

Russian Blue

Russian blues do hail from Russia, but for many years, they were known as Archangels because they were imported on ships from the Russian port of Archangel.

Their graceful body balances the slender Oriental shape (think Siamese) with the stocky shape of American shorthairs. Their double coat is short and always bright blue with a silver sheen. In some countries, white and black Russians are also bred.

Most authorities say these animals prefer a quiet life of routine. They're quite content hunkered down in a chair—soaking up the sun, their large ears almost translucent in the light.

Bombay

Named for the great black leopard of India, the Bombay is another human creation from about fifty years ago: Burmese cats were mated with black American shorthairs. Indeed, these elegant, compact, and strong cats do suggest a great cat in the wild. Even the way their back sways as they move resembles the confident swagger of a predator. Jet-black as a moonless night and good leash walkers and retrievers, Bombays can be great friends and playmates and are rarely wild or reckless.

Norwegian Forest Cat

Wegies (pronounced WEE-jeez) have roamed the forests of Norway since Viking times. Athletic outdoor types, these cats have been known to fish in creeks. Their long-haired, double-layered, rain-proof coat is even "accessorized" with tufted earmuffs, fluffy mittens, and a mane-like scarf framing the face.

Wegies love to be handled by family members but also love the independence of roaming and hunting outdoors. Uniquely, they can climb down trees, clinging to the bark with their claws. (Other cats can readily climb up, but either get stuck or jump down.)

British Shorthair

Though British shorthairs come in nearly every color and pattern, brilliant plush blue with large copper or gold eyes is the celebrated variety. A dignified, unfussy creature, this cat traces its ancestors back to Roman times.

Until 1871, this was simply the common street or household cat in Great Britain. But then a London cat fancier took one of these handsome, sturdy felines to its first cat show. Since that time, this breed, like the American shorthair, remains among the most popular pets. Perhaps it's their trainability. Or perhaps it's their muscular build, square body, and chubby cheeks—which have led them to be described as "the bulldog of cats."

American Shorthair

These are the cats the Pilgrims brought as mousers on their voyage to the New World. Breeding freely in America, they developed into robust, hearty creatures. Then, in the early twentieth century, breeders began to refine this animal, encouraging the popular tabby look that's now shown in an amazing thirty-four different colors and patterns.

The tabby camouflage—dark stripes on a lighter background—is the most familiar. Look for the M on the forehead: every tabby has one!

Burmese

This cat's origins date back to 1350 or 1767, depending on which confusing story you like better. The Burmese we know today traces its ancestry only to 1930s America—specifically, to a brief but tempestuous fling between an Oriental-type female and a seal-point Siamese. At first, all Burmese cats were sable colored: a rich brown. But now, champagne (or chocolate), blue, and platinum (or lilac) are standard.

Burmese cats don't like to be left alone. They're social creatures, happy with company, whether that's a stranger or someone in the family.

Birman

The sacred white-gloved cats of Myanmar (the small country also known as Burma) were once the beloved companions of temple priests. Our modern breed developed from a single pregnant individual brought to France and bred there. But fifty years ago, there were only two Birmans left in all of Europe, so those cats and their offspring were outbred, meaning that females were mated with males of a different breed to create a more diverse gene pool for healthier offspring.

Balinese

Named for the graceful temple dancers of Bali, a large Indonesian island situated between Southeast Asia and Australia, the Balinese is a longer-haired version of the Siamese—indeed, it used to be called the longhair Siamese. Since it has no undercoat, the Balinese's long and typically pale-colored topcoat feels especially silky.

Sporting a long, wedge-shaped head and almond-shaped, steel-blue eyes, the friendly Balinese is an acrobat and show-off. It needs to be center stage, with an active part in family life.

Himalayan

These cats are the result of some eighty years of breeding the slim, exotically colored Siamese with the stockier, long-haired Persian. Curiously, all Himalayans are born white; their points—the darker-colored ear tips, feet, and tail tip—show up within two weeks or so and continue to darken for a year and a half. Some cat registries call the Himalayan the color-point Persian. In Great Britain, this cat is called a color-point longhair. Still others know it as a Kashmir. Blue-eyed "sweet talkers," these cats have a soft, musical voice.

Japanese Bobtail

The bobtail, a white cat with another color or pattern on its body, is Japan's national cat. This treasured creature's ancestry goes back a thousand years or more; it's a part of Japan's national art and sculpture. Even now, ceramic cats called *maneki-neko* (mah-neh-kee-neh-koh) lift a paw to welcome visitors to stores and offer good luck in homes.

According to ancient tradition, bobtails possess the ability to perform sorcery. Reddish cats have the most power. White-brown-black mixes are second most powerful. Third place in the sorcery department goes to black-and-white cats.

Abyssinian

Perhaps the oldest breed of domestic cat, the Abyssinian carries the look of felines carved and painted in ancient Egyptian sculptures. It also resembles the wildcats of Africa, whose banded coat provides camouflage in the forests. With a slim, muscular body, the Aby has a regally arched neck, large almond eyes, and sizable ears.

Soft, silky, and ticked—that's when hairs have alternating bands of light and dark color—this cat's coat has invisible striping. Yes, it's a tabby! This kind of coat is called agouti, after a rodent with similarly color-banded fur.

Loyal, affectionate, but more climber than sitter, the Aby is athletic and determined to entertain you—or itself.

Persian

Known as the longhair in England, the Persian cat has been a beloved companion since the 1600s. But it's only in the last two hundred years that this cat, in its many colors and patterns, has come to resemble the animal we know today. Its very thick double coat has long, flowing guard hairs that can grow six inches long! (Quick lesson in cat fur: The undercoat is composed of down hairs—wool-like, short strands closest to the body—and awn hairs—bristly, longer strands. The topcoat is all guard hairs: longer, visible, silky strands.) The Persian shares with the Pekingese dog a distinctively shortened neck and a face that almost rests on the shoulders.

While Queen Victoria loved and cherished her Persians, she hardly outdid Florence Nightingale, who had sixty Persians in her lifetime.

In the haiku, I imagined the old cat, nearly deaf, in a world grown as quiet as the Persian's own quiet, well-mannered demeanor.

Havana Brown

For a hundred years, breeders tried to develop an all-brown cat. In the 1950s, a black Persian mated with a chocolate-point Siamese. The resulting kittens were called chestnut-brown foreign shorthairs.

This feline doesn't hail from Havana, Cuba, although some say that the cat's mahogany-cinnamon color, resembling the famous Cuban cigars, suggested its name. And I certainly imagine this poem's tropic heat set on that island. Sadly, the stray cat population in Cuba is overwhelming.

Interestingly, this is the only cat for which the breed standard specifies a whisker color. Yes, they must be brown to match the coat.

Scottish Fold

This unusual breed with ears that are folded down rather than pricked up arose from one cat born in Scotland in 1961. Not that this was the first time folded ears appeared on cats; it's a mutation mentioned throughout the records of feline history.

Scottish fold kittens are actually born with straight ears; it takes almost a month to see if each kitten will or won't express the gene for folded ears, will or won't enjoy the adoring comments of how it looks like an owl, a teddy bear, or a pixie.

Today, all colors and patterns, with a few exceptions, appear in the Scottish fold, and there are both short-haired and long-haired varieties. Though they possess a barn cat's confidence, they have the soft-spoken voice of a librarian.

Bengal

This spotted or marbled cat has wild blood in its veins: its ancestors were Asian leopard cats bred with domestic cats. Once known as the leopardette, the variety we know is the result of a rigid breeding program begun thirty years ago. Bengals have a broad head, wide muzzle, and larger whisker pads. Their large almond eyes are as attentive as a wildcat's.

To maintain that distinctive spotting, breeders need to reintroduce wildcats as mates every so many generations. Regrettably, that can cause cats to revert to undomesticated instincts such as guardedness, unpredictability, and unprovoked attacks. Fanciers may show only cats that are four generations away from a leopard cat parent; families are encouraged to observe this regulation as well.

Manx

The tail-less cat from the Isle of Man in the Irish Sea probably arose as a genetic problem that the isolated island allowed to increase. And since the Manx has been bred and shown for two centuries, you can now find Manx cats in nearly all colors and patterns.

This cat is round in nearly every way: body, eyes, rump, head, paws. They walk with a "bunny hop" movement because of their longer hind legs.

Fetching or burying toys, perching in the highest places, speedily running the circuit of the house, the Manx is a clowning, owner-loving character, full of intelligence.

For my mother, who gave me everything
as a child . . . as a grown-up, but a cat

M. J. R.

For Edwin, a great artist and friend

L. W.

Text copyright © 2015 by Michael J. Rosen
Illustrations copyright © 2015 by Lee White

First edition 2015

Library of Congress Catalog Card Number 2013957344
ISBN 978-0-7636-6492-3

14 15 16 17 18 19 CCP 10 9 8 7 6 5 4 3 2 1
Printed in Shenzhen, Guangdong, China

This book was typeset in Journal and Bookeyed Suzanne.
The illustrations were created digitally.

Candlewick Press
99 Dover Street
Somerville, Massachusetts 02144

visit us at www.candlewick.com